Robin Hood Meets Little John

D0898710

Retold by Jenny Giles

Illustrated by John Fairbridge

Chapter One

Robin and His Merry Men

Long, long ago, a band of outlaws lived in Sherwood Forest, near the town of Nottingham, in England. They were well known throughout the land for their hunting skills and their fearless deeds. The most famous outlaw of all was the leader of these merry men, Robin Hood.

Most of the time, Robin and his men stayed hidden in the great forest, so that the Sheriff of Nottingham would not find them.

The sheriff was a cruel man, who treated the poor farmers very badly. He often sent his soldiers to terrify them, and to take all the crops that they had worked so hard to grow. Many of the farmers did not have enough food left for their families.

3

The sheriff was determined to catch Robin Hood, because he and the other outlaws took money from the rich people who rode through Sherwood Forest. Some of these rich people were the sheriff's friends, and they were furious with Robin, because he gave their money to the poor farmers so that they would not starve.

But the outlaws were too clever for the sheriff and his soldiers. They always managed to escape to the hideout that they had made for themselves, deep within the forest.

Chapter Two

The Challenge

One fine day, when Robin and several of his men were walking beside a stream, they heard the sound of someone approaching.

"Quick!" muttered Robin. "Hide behind the trees! One of the sheriff's men may be looking for us."

But it was not a soldier who was walking on the other side of the stream. It was a tall stranger, and in his hand he held a staff made from a straight, narrow branch. The outlaws could see that he was about to step onto the trunk of a fallen tree, which was used as a bridge over the water.

"Stay here," said Robin to his men. "I will ask this stranger what he is doing in Sherwood Forest."

As Robin stepped onto the bridge, the stranger stared at him in surprise and shouted, "Move aside! I wish to cross this stream."

"And so do I," answered Robin. "But there is not enough room for both of us. You will have to go back onto the river bank."

8

The stranger frowned. "I stepped onto this bridge before you," he said, "and I shall cross over it before you. Now, get out of my way!" He took a pace forward.

"Stay where you are!" shouted Robin. "We shall settle this matter in a fair fight. But first, I will need a staff. Wait there while I cut one for myself."

"I will gladly wait," replied the stranger, "so that I may then have the great pleasure of knocking you into the stream."

Robin put down his longbow and his arrows, and went to a nearby tree. He cut a strong, narrow branch, and trimmed it quickly. Then he returned to face the stranger.

Step by step, the two men moved carefully along the bridge, each with his staff raised in front of him.

"This stranger is one of the tallest and strongest men I have ever seen," thought Robin. "I am beginning to wonder if I should have challenged him to a fight."

But Robin was a brave man, and very skilled at using a staff. He continued to move along the bridge, watching the stranger closely.

Suddenly, the stranger hit Robin's staff with a powerful blow. Robin almost slipped, but as he regained his footing he lifted his staff and swung it down sharply.

The stranger was ready for him. He swayed to one side, and then attacked again.

The two men stepped back and forth, but neither would give way. As the fight went on, it seemed that there would be no winner.

Then the stranger lifted his staff high above his head, and took a great stride forward. He hit Robin's staff with such force that it broke in two.

Robin was caught off balance, and he staggered. Then he slipped off the bridge and fell into the stream.

Chapter Three

Little John Joins the Outlaws

The outlaws came running out of the forest to help Robin.

"Wait!" he shouted to them. "This man has beaten me in a fair fight, and so we must let him cross the bridge. And besides, we need another strong fellow to join us."

The outlaws waited as the stranger walked across the bridge. They watched in silence as Robin waded out of the stream.

"I am Robin Hood," he declared to the stranger. "Would you join me and my band of merry men, and help us in our fight against the cruel Sheriff of Nottingham?"

"I have heard many stories of the great Robin Hood!" replied the stranger. "Your name is known far and wide, and I would like nothing better than to join you!"

"Then tell us your name," said Robin.

"I am called John Little," replied the stranger, and he smiled as he spoke.

"Indeed, I know why you smile!" said Robin, and he chuckled. "You are surely the tallest and strongest man I have ever met! I think we should call you 'Little John' from now on!"

"Little John I shall be," agreed the stranger, as he shook the hand of each outlaw.

"And to celebrate, we shall have a great feast," declared Robin Hood, "so that we may all welcome our new friend, Little John, to Sherwood Forest."